Winston 500

by Eric Ethan

Gareth Stevens Publishing
MILWAUKEE

The author wishes to thank Glen Fitzgerald, George Philips, Mary Jo Lindahl, and Juanita Jones for their help and encouragement.

For a free color catalog describing Gareth Stevens Publishing's list of high-quality books and multimedia programs, call 1-800-542-2595 (USA) or 1-800-461-9120 (Canada). Gareth Stevens Publishing's Fax: (414) 225-0377.

Library of Congress Cataloging-in-Publication Data

Ethan, Eric.
    Winston 500 / by Eric Ethan.
        p. cm. — (NASCAR! an imagination library series)
    Includes index.
    Summary: Describes the action at the Winston 500, held at the Talladega Superspeedway in Alabama.
    ISBN 0-8368-2141-6 (lib. bdg.)
    1. Winston 500 (Automobile race)—Juvenile literature.   2. Stock car racing—Juvenile literature.   [1. Winston 500 (Automobile race).   2. Stock car racing.]   I. Title.   II. Series: Ethan, Eric.   NASCAR! an imagination library series.
    GV1033.5.W56E85   1999
    796.72'06'876161—dc21   99-24779

First published in North America in 1999 by
Gareth Stevens Publishing
1555 North RiverCenter Drive, Suite 201
Milwaukee, WI 53212 USA

This edition © 1999 by Gareth Stevens, Inc. Text by Eric Ethan. Photographs © 1998: Cover, pp. 5, 7, 11, 13, 15, 17, 19, 21 - Don Grassman. Illustration: p. 9 - The Official NASCAR Preview and Press Guide. Additional end matter © 1999 by Gareth Stevens, Inc.

Text: Eric Ethan
Page layout: Lesley M. White
Cover design: Lesley M. White
Editorial assistant: Diane Laska

Printed in the United States of America

1 2 3 4 5 6 7 8 9 03 02 01 00 99

TABLE OF CONTENTS

Metric Chart

1 mile = 1.609 kilometers	1 foot = .3048 meter
100 miles = 160.9 km	4,000 feet = 1,219.2 m
500 miles = 804.5 km	

Words that appear in the glossary are printed in
boldface type the first time they occur in the text.

THE WINSTON 500

The Winston 500 is one of thirty-two races **sanctioned** by the National Association for Stock Car Auto Racing (NASCAR). It has been held annually in mid-October since 1970. The Winston 500 is the largest sporting event in Alabama. Drivers travel around the track a total of 500 miles to complete the race, which lasts several hours. Over 155,000 people watch the Winston 500 at the racetrack each year, making it one of the biggest of all the NASCAR events.

Champion drivers Dale Earnhardt, Davey Allison, Cale Yarborough, and Richard Petty have all raced in the Winston 500. In 1985, Bill Elliott set the average-speed record of 186.288 miles per hour. He also set the single-lap speed record in 1987 — an amazing 212.809 miles per hour!

4

*This photograph shows the view from the **starter's** flag stand during the 1998 Winston Cup race.*
CIA Stock Photo: Don Grassman

TALLADEGA SUPERSPEEDWAY

The Winston 500 race is held at the Talladega Superspeedway in Talladega, Alabama, east of Birmingham. The superspeedway, which opened in 1969, cost over $4 million to build. At first, it was named the Alabama International Motor Speedway.

The Talladega Superspeedway was the dream of William H. G. France, Sr., founder of NASCAR. France called people together for the first NASCAR organizational meeting in 1947 in Daytona Beach, Florida. Millions of racing fans have visited the Talladega Superspeedway since it was built. Seating has been expanded every year for the last ten years. It can now seat 100,000 guests and accommodate thousands more in the 215-acre infield.

Stock cars head into a **banked** turn at the Talladega Superspeedway.
CIA Stock Photo: Don Grassman

THE TRACK

Talladega's track is a 2.66-mile tri-oval. A tri-oval has three large cornering areas. The track is four lanes wide, giving the cars plenty of room to run at top speed. The longest straightaway is 4,000 feet, and cars can reach speeds of over 200 miles per hour before they have to slow for the turn.

The three straightaways at Talladega are level, but the corners are banked. This means the track surface is tilted up on the outside. Banking increases a track's safety and allows the cars to go faster. Without it, the cars would have to travel much slower or they might fly off the track as they corner.

This diagram shows the tri-oval shape of the Talladega Superspeedway.
The Official NASCAR Preview and Press Guide

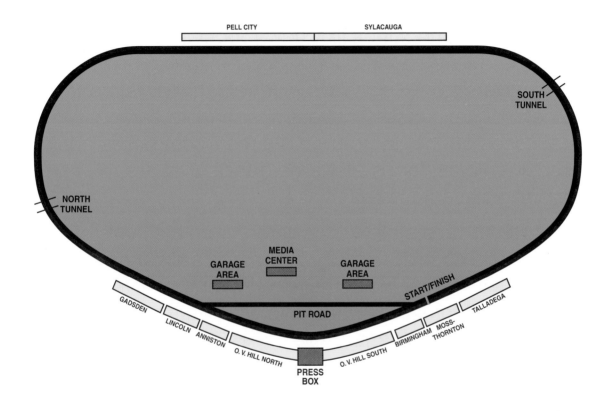

PELL CITY

SYLACAUGA

SOUTH
TUNNEL

NORTH
TUNNEL

MEDIA
CENTER

GARAGE
AREA

GARAGE
AREA

START/FINISH

GADSDEN

LINCOLN

ANNISTON

O. V. HILL NORTH

PIT ROAD

O.V. HILL SOUTH

BIRMINGHAM

MOSS-
THORNTON

TALLADEGA

PRESS
BOX

	TRACK FACILITIES
	SEATING
	INFIELD

TALLADEGA SUPERSPEEDWAY

Distance: *2.66 Miles*

Banking: *33 degrees*

Qualifying Record: *Bill Elliott, 212.809 mph (44.998 seconds), set April 30, 1987*

Race Record (500 Miles): *Bill Elliott, 186.288 mph, set May 5, 1985*

NASCAR RACERS

NASCAR racers look like new-model stock cars except they are covered with **logos**. Racing is a very expensive sport. **Sponsors** give racing teams money to help pay expenses. In return, sponsors can put their logos on the car to promote their companies and products. Most logos are large decals that are carefully placed onto each car.

NASCAR racers are very different from the kinds of cars people have at home. The frames are handmade. Passenger compartments have room for the driver only and are built for safety, not comfort. Drivers are protected by a **roll cage** made of heavy metal tubing that surrounds the driver's seat.

Bobby Labonte drove car 18, sponsored by Interstate Batteries, in the 1998 Winston Cup.
CIA Stock Photo: Don Grassman

SAFETY

Because of the high speeds reached during races, driver safety is a major concern. All race cars have special fuel **bladders** in their gas tanks. This helps keep the fuel from spilling onto the track if the car has an accident. Sometimes, in bad accidents, gas still leaks and fires break out. A fire extinguisher and an emergency air supply are available to each driver. In addition, each driver wears safety gear, such as fire-retardant clothes and a special helmet.

NASCAR regulates how a car must be built. This guarantees that no car has an unfair advantage over others and that all of them can go nearly as far or as fast on a single tank of gas. Qualities that create exciting NASCAR races and winning drivers are driver skill and efficient **pit stops**.

Special safety equipment is very important when cars drive close together at high speed.
CIA Stock Photo: Don Grassman

13

DALE JARRETT, WINNER

Dale Jarrett won the 1998 Winston 500. His team was sponsored by Quality Car Care/Ford Credit Foreland. Robert Yates owns the car. During the 1998 season, Jarrett won 3 of the 33 Winston Cup series races. He was third among all NASCAR drivers in the point standings at the end of the 1998 season.

Drivers are assigned points based on where they finish each race. They can win money for their teams if they are one of the top-placed finishers. Over his fourteen-year career, Jarrett has won more than $14 million.

Dale Jarrett's car number 88 won the 1998 Winston 500.
CIA Stock Photo: Don Grassman

QUALIFYING

Before drivers can compete in a race, they must **qualify**. Qualifying takes place a few days before the race and is a very important part of winning. Usually, in a qualifying lap, a single driver is on the track at one time. The goal is to drive once around the track as fast as possible. When all the drivers have tried to qualify, race officials decide the starting order of the race. The fastest car is awarded the **pole** position. This is in the front row on the inside. Slower cars line up farther back. Most NASCAR races allow only about forty cars to enter. Since the number of entrants is limited, cars that don't go fast enough aren't allowed to race. Race mechanics use qualifying as a chance to do some engine tuning so their car runs well on each particular racetrack.

Dale Earnhardt, Chad Little, and Jeff Gordon battle for position during the 1998 Winston 500.
CIA Stock Photo: Don Grassman

RACE DAY

When the starter drops the green flag, all the cars roar down the straightaway. Cars in the pole position and the first few rows have an advantage at the start of the race because there is less traffic ahead of them, and they can go full speed.

During the race, cars are often very close together. Staying close behind another car lowers wind resistance for the second car. In this way, the car that is behind uses less fuel than the one in front. This is called **drafting**. Drivers try to balance going fast with not being destructive to their cars. Collisions can quickly take a car out of a race. It requires skill and courage to drive in a group of tightly packed cars at 150 miles per hour!

Driver Ken Schrader's car was damaged in an accident during the 1998 Winston 500.
CIA Stock Photo: Don Grassman

PIT ACTION

Changing tires and refueling the car quickly during a pit stop means possibly getting back onto the racetrack faster than a competitor.

Pit crews wait behind a low safety wall until their car comes to a full stop in front of them. Then the entire crew leaps over the wall and goes to work. Prizes are given each year to the best pit crews because they are such an important part of every race.

When a car has a minor accident or a breakdown, pit mechanics are responsible for getting the car fixed and back into the race. The car might go slower, but it will finish. Finishing a race is important, even if the car doesn't win, because the team receives points.

Driver Rusty Wallace's pit crew springs into action during the 1998 Winston 500.
CIA Stock Photo: Don Grassman

ACCIDENTS

Accidents are an unfortunate part of NASCAR racing. Most drivers are very competitive, and they want to win. Large cash purses and powerful race cars combine to make a dangerous sport. Part of the excitement of a race is knowing that drivers bravely face these risks during a race.

NASCAR has worked to control the risks and emphasizes safe races, while still keeping the thrill and excitement. Modern tracks are better designed than ever before, as are modern race cars. Drivers spend many years developing their skills before they reach the top races. They all accept risk as a necessary and unavoidable part of the job and their dream of becoming a NASCAR winner.

GLOSSARY

You can find these words on the pages listed. Reading a word in a sentence helps you understand it even better.

banked — inclined upward from the inside edge 6

bladders (BLAD-ers) — sacks that hold a liquid, such as gasoline 12

drafting (DRAF-ting) — when one car follows closely behind another during a race to save fuel and engine wear 18

logos (LOW-gos) — graphic designs that feature the name or product of a company 10

pit stops — time-outs from a car race when a car goes to the side of the track where team members attend to it 12, 20

pole — the inside, front spot in a car race 16, 18

qualify (KWAH-lih-fy) — pass a test that makes a person or object fit for a certain position 9, 16

roll cage — a framework of metal bars that encloses and protects a race car driver 10

sanctioned (SANK-shunned) — approved by an official group 4

sponsors (SPON-sers) — companies that pay money to support something 10, 14

starter — a person who signals the beginning of a race 4, 18

stock cars — new-model sedans manufactured by Detroit automakers, such as Ford, General Motors, and Chevrolet 4, 10

PLACES TO WRITE

International Motor Sports Museum
Public Relations Manager
3198 Speedway Boulevard
Talladega, AL 35160

Daytona USA
Public Relations Manager
1801 West International Boulevard
Daytona Beach, FL 32114

Motorbooks International
Public Relations Manager
729 Prospect Avenue/Box 1
Osceola, WI 54020

Rick Humphrey, Public Relations Director
Talladega Superspeedway
P.O. Box 777
Talladega, AL 35161

WEB SITES

www.nascar.com

This is the official web site of the National Association for Stock Car Auto Racing.

www.ciastockphoto.com

This is one of the best NASCAR photo sites. It is the source of many of the pictures in this book. It presents new images during each racing season.

racing.yahoo.com/rac/nascar

At this web site, race fans can find current NASCAR race results, standings, schedules, driver profiles, feature stories, and merchandise.

Due to the dynamic nature of the Internet, some web sites stay current longer than others. To find additional web sites, use a reliable search engine with one or more of the following keywords: *Bill Elliott, William H. G. France, Sr., Dale Jarrett, NASCAR, Talladega Superspeedway, Rusty Wallace,* and *Winston 500.*

INDEX